HER THOUGHTS!

A collection of meaningful poems and reflections!

DEZARITA DASHAI

Her Thoughts!

A collection of meaningful poems and reflections!

By Dezarita Dashai

Cover Designed by Jazzy Kitty Publications

Published by Jazzy Kitty Publications

Logo Designed by LeRoy Grayson

Editor: Anelda L. Attaway

© 2022 Dezarita Dashai

ISBN 978-1-954425-53-8

Library of Congress Control Number: 2022911187

A collection of meaningful poems and reflections!

DEDICATION

I dedicate this small collection of poems and reflections to all the folks in the world that has begun their healing process. LET IT OUT!

*DEZARITA DASHAI *

TABLE OF CONTENTS

INTRODUCTION

For so long I sat with my thoughts in my head as they gave me constant anxiety and depression.

Pushing them back, ignoring them...hoping they disappear. Sound familiar?

I was afraid to speak on anything for so many reasons.

Folks have their own burdens to bear; I am being too dramatic. Does anyone really care?

My thoughts turned into feelings that weighed my soul down as I kept it all in.

We wear a smile as if we are all good, but deep inside we are hurting.

This is because we had not gotten a hold of our thoughts. We must feel it to get past it!

Turning to unhealthy coping skills is not going to make the thoughts go away!

Come join me as I start this amazing journey of healing as we reflect on "her thoughts!"

Who knows they may happen to be a thought or two of yours as well.

Our thoughts soon will be released from our souls and before we know it!

WE WILL BE FREE!

Write it out, sing it out, or even scream it out

Just please!

LET IT OUT!

Ready to reflect on "her thoughts?"

Let's go!!!

CLARITY

I PRAY FOR CLARITY!

Not to be in Love or Rich or even the Baddish Bitch

CLARITY-CLARITY CLA-RI-TY!

You see sometimes our Eyes Deceive us!

Our Minds, Oh Yes, it plays Tricks on us

Meeting you....You were all I ever Needed

You were my High as I so ever Feened it!

As time Passes, my Vision of you Blurs...

My mind becomes a Live Circus, as thoughts I Entertain

All compete for my Undivided Attention

SO YES, I PRAY FOR CLARITY!

CLARITY, CLARITY, CLA-RI-TY!

That God Himself can take away this new Doubt called Fear

Pull my Eyes to the Front instead of the Rear.

To be able to take off my "DESIRE" of your Lens

So that I can really see you up until the Very End!

No more making my Body Tense after I've made a Decision

Got my Soul Stuck, fighting for Revision.

Causing such an Uproar in my Heart!

I promise this is the hardest Fucking part

I PRAY FOR CLARITY

CLARITY, CLARITY, CLA-RA-TY!

As I Meditate and Manifest all that's Mine!

I give thanks because, Honey, I am One of a Kind!

I choose to see you through Glasses of your highest self

To Disregard your Lowest of the Lows

I choose to fight a Million thoughts in my Head

Without a Win!

To Love all of you!

Through and Through

Beginning, Middle, and End!

My Heart is made of Gold,

It will be this way beyond my grey and old

CLARITY, CLARITY, CLA-RI-TY!

As the Fog Settles in my Mind

My Heart develops a Constant Pattern again

My Soul Smiles as I thank God for such Revelation!

CLARITY, CLARITY, CLA-RI-TY

Don't let the Uneasy Chills from others Freeze your Heart

Just do your Part and Pray for

CLARITY-CLARITY, CLA-RI-TY!

REFLECTION

A cluttered mind isn't worth a damn!

What is something you would like to get clarity about?

Have you gone to your higher power about it?

Let's Write it out!

Below answer all questions.

How does not having clarity about something or someone make you feel?'

Are you operating at your best without the clarity you seek? If not, what has that cost you?

List three things that you can do for yourself to gain clarity!

Give yourself time! You will receive some wonderful

CLARITY, CLARITY, CLA-RI-TY!

_____

_____

_____

_____

_____

IF I COULD

IF I COULD

I'd Fly Away from here

To nowhere, but Everywhere

I'D FLY, FLY, FLY AWAY FROM HERE!

IF I COULD

I'd falls In Love with you

Have you thinking about Me and Only Me boo!

When you close your Eyes, I'd have you Mesmerized

By my glorious Smile as it welcomes you countless

Rays of Sunshine

ONLY IF I COULD

I WOULD

IF I COULD

If I could, I'd sneak off with you

Wed explore all parts of our Bodies

The Good, Bad, Old and New

Releasing yelps of Pleasure and Excitement.

I'd Sneak,

Sneak away.

Sneak AWAY with you!

ONLY IF I COULD,

I WOULD

IF I COULD!

WHEN YOU SAY YOU LOVE ME

WHEN YOU SAY YOU LOVE ME,

What part of ME is it?

Because as my Thoughts turn, my Sleepless Nights

Into Tearful Showers

I HEAR YOUR WORDS

"I LOVE YOU"

But do you really?

The me whose Struggles get the best of her,

So, she Shuts Down, going Ghost

Not wanting or needing anyone around

Do you Love Me for what or who I am?

What I am is a Complicated Melody

Needing High Vibrations and ONLY Good Energy!

Are you certain you Love Me?"

No longer will I Fuss and Fight for you to get it Right

It's all up to you to do exactly what you need to do!

You can't Kiss or Hug me for a Quick Thrill.

You must connect Deep within my Soul,

So, I know it's Real.

I HEAR YOUR WORDS

"I LOVE YOU!"

But do you really?

What I am!

Is a Strong, Beautiful BLACK QUEEN!

One who chases after ALL her Dreams!

Resilience is her Name!

She's always ahead of the Game!

Are you sure you LOVE ME?

Am I too Independent for your Taste?

You must understand I Attract

And NEVER Chase!

As I Walk my Walk

I listen to you Talk your Talk

"I LOVE YOU!"

But do you really?

I AM WHO AND WHAT I AM!

If you Love Me, SHOW IT!

Because all that Talking Ain't Worth a Damn!

REFLECTION

It's important to know what your Love language is so you can

verbally express the best way to be loved!

Do you feel Loved by the folks in your Life?

Why or Why not?

What is your Love Language?

Why do you feel that is?

_____

_____

_____

_____

_____

_____

_____

_____

_____

_____

_____

_____

_____

_____

Her Thoughts!

Dezarita Dashai

WOULD YOU LET ME LOVE?

WOULD YOU LET ME LOVE YOU?

No! I mean like...REALLY Love you?

Let me run your Bath Water after a long day of Work.

If you need It. I got it

We will never be broke!

Let me feed not just your Belly but your Soul

Honey, my Heart is FULL OF GOLD!

Thirsty? Let me quench that Thirst

With my Strawberry Milkshake!

Listen! I can't sing a Lic!

But, won't ya let me sing to ya!

Cuz baybe *"you mean the world to me,*

You are my everything, I swear, the only thing that matters.

BAYBEE!

Won't you let my Soft, Sweet, Succulent Lips meet yours!

I want to Whisper Words of Motivation in your Ear

As I climb on top of your Mountain!

No hesitation needed!

All of your Inch's slide into my Tight Space

Yet, I NEVER STOP Caressing your Face!

My Waves rush out, Saturating all parts in their way

1 after the other as I continue to Ride

Round and Round and Round

Stopping in Mid-Stroke

Still awaiting your response!

WOULD YOU LET ME LOVE YOU?

No! I mean, like REALLY LOVE YOU?

WOULD YOU?

I, AM, SORRY!

I'M SORRY!

I'm sorry,

I didn't show you the Love you needed to be okay.

Hiding Words that could have helped take the Pain Away

I'M SORRY!

I'm sorry

I held back the Worth that you didn't know you had

But needed Oh So Very Bad

Kicking you while you Down as you lounged in Self Pity

Allowing you to run away from Me-to Flee-

To become someone else-JUST TO BE!

I, AM, SORRY!

I'M SORRY!

I'm sorry,

I let you become a Doormat to this World

So Scared to let you use your Voice!

Independent all day long is still my Ultimate Choice!

But you must know that we are LOVED

WE ARE WANTED WE ARE ENOUGH!

Hanging my Head Down Low

I LET IT ALL GO

I look you in your Eyes as I take off all my Disguises

OEEE HONEY,

I Am So Sorry that I hurt you!

PLEASE, PLEASE, PLEASE!

Accept my Swaying Tears as I lay down my Soul

Surrendering!

Let's lay our Wounded Hearts Down

I'd make our Life Better

Yes! You and I!

We can Heal together

Although our Conversation has shifted into a

Different Direction

I am still staring at my own reflection!

Dezarita Dashai

I'm so Sorry that I hurt you!

But come on now, let's push through

BECAUSE WE HAVE A WHOLE LOT OF

LIVIN' LIFE TO DO!

REFLECTION

We are the #1 person who hurts ourselves

What are you sorry to yourself for?

Write a letter to yourself expressing your apology,

then connect deep within yourself and tell yourself

I AM SORRY!

THERE IS NO BETTER LOVE THAN SELF-LOVE!

_____

_____

_____

_____

_____

_____

_____

_____

_____

_____

_____

Her Thoughts!

THE MAN SHE WANTS HIM TO BE

THE MAN SHE WANTS HIM TO BE

Is the man he Use to Be

So to say!

One who Rescued her Broken Heart and helped

MEND THEM ALL BACK TOGETHER AGAIN!

The man she wants him to be isn't Intimidated by

Her Strong Structure of Independency

He allows it to Motivate him to go HARDER!

Leading correctly as his Masculine Energy Flows

Yet knows when to open up

AND LET ALL THAT SHIT GO!

THE MAN SHE WANTS HIM TO BE

Is the man he Use to Be

So to say!

If he could just be the man to meet her Halfway

Then she will Commit to Making Love to him

Every Single Day!

Be so involved in your children's lives

Any absence of you shows up on their Face

You're a King

Walk like it with Grace!

THE MAN SHE WANTS HIM TO BE

Is indeed the man

HE should Strive to Be!

YOU SEE, THE MAN SHE WANTS HIM TO BE

Is no longer a Want-but a Need!

She Feens him, she Craves him

So much

That when she Closes her Eyes

She sees herself with him!

Together at last, as he holds here in his Soul

A Peace comes over her, making her feel Whole

But when she Opens her Eyes

THERE HE STANDS!

THE MAN SHE NEEDS HIM TO BE

Is still not the man

He Use to Be

So to say!

Welp!

Ya know what Queens say

It's her way or the Highway...

DUCES!!!!

IT CAN'T WIN

Two aching legs

Relying on these ten Tremulous Fingers to assist them Budge

But oh no, they insist on demanding my mind to Pacify itself

To get a hold on to this Dis-Belief

And Focus on the Here and Now

REALITY!

My mind, in return Weeps out for my Heart to do its part

And Integrate them all back together again!

Even then!

IT CAN'T WIN!

There lies my Soul in Pieces

So helplessly calling out for a Deposit of Love

In any Way, Shape or Form.

Longing to be Refilled, Restored

Put back together again!

My Heart is now Vacant!

Feelings NO LONGER Occupy it!

My Mind is filled with Meaningful Memories

Of you, of I, of us!

To receive an Oz of Love back in return,

Was all I ever yearned for.

Fatigue takes over my body

From the inside out!

I'm drained,

weary,

beat

I AM EMPTY!

My Legs and Fingers form into my Ahsana

The heavy shades over my Eyes fall shut gaining Moisture

Under the Moonlight

I start to feel alright

The Tension I felt all within my form

Begins to sense.

I melt off unto the Dark Sky

For I know

I am Light!

The Stars, Twinkle in my Soul,

Slowly making me whole.

Breath in, Breath out

A Healthy Balance of give and take

Is what it's all about!

REFLECTION

Did you know that your Mind, Heart, and Soul can experience fatigue?

So often, we pour into other cups repeatedly, yet we allow our cup to run dry!

We are to live Life in overflow so that we can pour into others with ease!

Do you find yourself running low on love, patience, of simply being able to help?

Take a moment to write out what caused you to fill that way.

Create boundaries to prevent it from happening again!

But, most importantly, take a moment to RECHARGE in whatever form that looks like for you!

_____

_____

_____

_____

_____

_____

I WANT IT!

I WANT IT!

IT!

It halts my Anxiety and just lets me be!

My Smile is not Forced but pleasantly Present!

IT!

It sends Chills of Acceptance as I bask in its Presence!

Shoulders Down, jaws Unclenched

Feel the Heat from my Hands, touch my Thighs

AWARE!

Capture the Coldness from the Floor as it Chills My Feet

Calm!

IT!

I WANT IT!

It welcomes my Rainstorm Full of Tears

Stays with me beyond my Greatest Fears!

There is NOTHING like it, you see

Wherever it is at, it's where I got to be!

IT!

It makes my World okay

As all my Anxiety fades away!

I WANT IT!

IT!

It is a high Unreachable, a destination Undiscoverable!

I WANT IT!

IT!

I JUST DO!

PLEASE OH PLEASE

COULD YOU WANT ME TOO!

I Dreamed of this beautiful young lady

Oh, but baby am I Her?

You see, I have to ask,

Because she appeared to have this Confident Demeanor

About her.

It said: I AM THE SHIT!

It said: FUCK YOU!

It said: Hate it or Love it...THIS IS ME!

Am I HER?

Nawl, I'm always second-guessing myself...

Kissing Ass...diming down my Light,

For You, You and YOU!

Allowing my Boundaries to Moved,

By Assholes, who see my Heart and

Choose to Abuse it!

Oh, but not this Lil Lady!

She stood on her Nos

And stood up for her Yess!

I looked in the mirror

Damn! Am I HER?

Oeeee Weeee, my skin Glowed as hers did.

My eyes Twinkle with such Sass!

My Smile called out to my Soul and Snatched it up

As it yelled

YES!

YOU ARE HER!

Now stand up and be HER!

YOUR CONFIDENT...

TAP INTO IT!

AS YOU SHINE LIKE THE DIAMOND YOU ARE

REMEMBER YOUR YES MEANS YES

AND NO MEANS NO!

BABY, YOU ARE DEFINITELY HER!

CALL HER BY HER NAME #QUEENDEZARITA

REFLECTION

Do you ever see the person you want to be in your dreams?

Do you hear the things you want to say float around your head, but they just will not slide off your Tongue? Do you have a list of goals you're afraid you can't reach?

Take a moment and reflect on how these questions make you feel. Give thought to the person inside of you, longing to be seen. Figure out how you can let that person be!

Because that my friend is who you are, and one should never hide who they are. But tap into it and become one with it!

YES, HONEY YOU ARE HER AND SHE IS YOU!

_____

_____

_____

_____

_____

_____

_____

_____

_____

Her Thoughts!

ON THE EDGE

I swear I am Full of Love

No Cap!

But here lately,

I'VE BEEN ON THE EDGE OF FUCK AND YOU!

So, your best bet is to Leave Me Alone Boo!

My words now get lost Traveling

From my Mind to my Lips.

When I look at you

Hope Evaporates, my Pressure Rises

And my Emotions Race!

Keep on dismissing my Request without Hesitation

I've been done requiring your Validation

Help yourself to my empty touches of Affection

I have NOTHING MORE to Give

And you!

You have Nothing for me to Take!

Yup!

You have pushed me

TO THE EDGE OF

FUCK AND YOU!

Please, Please, Please

Keep your non-changing

Non-effective Sorriest Sorry.

Save your One-Time Efforts of Making a Change

No need to Force yourself

To be someone you're not!

It's plain to see,

The water isn't Boiling

Just sitting in the Pot.

Hell, I have got to make a Change

Before my Actions turn beyond Strange!

I AM CLEARLY ON THE EDGE OF

FUCK AND YOU!

If I NO LONGER Serve you,

And you NO LONGER Serve me.

Let's just Let Go of each other

So, we can Simply Be!

We have to just Walk Away from this Boo!

Because I am telling you!

I AM ON THE EDGE OF

FUCK AND YOU!

WE HAVE FINISHED THE RACE

Ever want to Run, run as Fast as you can?

Simply disappear for a Moment or Two.

Hoping when you Return, your Problems will be All Through.

Ever think: man, what am I doing Wrong?

Am I causing my own Downfalls?

Each night we have to Pray,

Lord Our God

Please show us the way.

What more is there to do? What more is there to Say?

Ever feel like you're Buried under tons and tons of Dismay?

We break thru and keep on Moving,

Only to be Glued to the Ground

Yet time keeps on a Grooving!

Never give up they say!

You're Strong, you will make it thru someway.

Ever feel completely Stuck between a Rock and a Hard Place?

Of course, Life is one Hell of a Race!

However, we must Push Through and give it our Best,

Not paying any mind to the Rest.

Do you ever feel the Entire World

Has crumbled over you?

Asking a Million Questions

Like why you?

As long as we keep Moving,

We can almost see the Finish Line

No matter how many Times

We get Flat Lined.

We will always Come Back!

Oh Yes! It is a known Fact!

Yes, we feel like Bump Life!

We are tired,

And will NEVER get it Right.

Well, just Step Out on your Faith and

Before you know it

You will be Thanking God

Because of His Mercy and His Grace

Look at us yawl!

WE HAVE FINISHED THE RACE!

REFLECTION

Life gives us so many races, one after another.

How do you feel when Life gives you lemons?

Are they healthy options?

If not, how can you take the first step to gaining healthy outlets.

Do you have healthy coping techniques? If so, what are they?

_____

_____

_____

_____

_____

_____

_____

_____

_____

_____

_____

_____

_____

MAYBE

MAYBE

Maybe, I should let my Tears Race Down without Disruption.

Give authorization for them to Cleanse My Heart

And wash it New,

I NEED A REDO

A FRESH START!

Because clearly, I WANT NO PARTS!

Maybe this here Heart is for the Birds

A LESSON LEARNED

Maybe I want to Kick this suckka to the Curb

AND LET IT ALL FUCKIN' BURN!

MAYBE!!!

Maybe my New Heart can get a hold to the Permeant Detour

My Life has taken.

Live Life without expecting any Fairytale Endings

Hell, all of mine were Mistaken.

MAYBE

I can be as Cold and Bold as some of these folks in the World.

A Harden Heart

Simply doing its Part!

MAYBE!!!

Maybe there will be no more Pardon me

And somehow, my Mouth will Halt

All those sad 'ol Sorrys!

MAYBE HUH!

MAYBE!

TUUUUHHHH!

How about I just let my Heart be

And tell all, you No Good Jokers

If you can't Love and Accept me for me

Stay away from this Beautiful person

Known as a Queen!!!!!

MAYBE HUH?

MAYBE!!!!!

SOMEWHERE ALONG THE WAY

Somewhere along the Earths constant Slow Spin

LIFE became Life!

When did it become a Crime to be a kid?

To Sag?

Or consider yourself to have the most Swag,

Without being called a Fag or Delinquent?

When did it become okay to Pronounce them Guilty

With your Guns and your Badge,

Just because you think it.

Yet, you get rewarded with No Convictions of such

But Low-Key getting Handshakes from the Mayor

Like you did a Bunch!

SOMEWHERE ALONG THE LINE

We became Ok with just being "Niggas"

SOMEWHERE ALONG THE LINE

We lost the Determination, Motivation

For Peace, for Love, for EQUALITY!

The Blood our Ancestors shed day in and day out

Somehow "Evaporated"

When did we become okay with Killing each other?

Laying down our rights as Black Americans?

SOMEWHERE ALONG THE LINE

We became Weak, Selfish and Pathetic

As the Clouds grow Thicker and the Sky sinks Lower

You have no choice but to open your eyes

OPEN THEM!

See how somewhere along the way

KIDS

Real true definition of kids

Became Extinct!

No more yes Sirs and no Mams

No more Family Dinners where

Kids picked the Greens and peeled the Yams

There is no such thing as kids staying in a Kid's Place

Because they are all growing up

At too much of a Fast Pace!

Somewhere along the way

Parents stop being parents

BUT FRIENDS

Putting the meaning of

Love, Teaching, and Discipline

To a Horrible End!

Somewhere along the way

Us being whole

Became lost from Deep within our Soul.

We were made to love as thy self!

Our purpose is to live at Peace

Under God's will. Not our own.

Somewhere along the way

Mannnn, we really Messed up

But if we pull together, we can Erupt

And get it All Right!

Somewhere along the way

We must step back

Surrender

And let God lead the way

Before IT'S WAY TO LATE!

REFLECTION

Thinking back to being around your grandparents as a child vs. Now.

What do you see different? WHAT DO YOU SEE THE SAME?

Is it possible for us to return to those same traditions?

Why or why not?

_____

_____

_____

_____

_____

_____

_____

_____

_____

_____

_____

IN PLAIN SIGHT

If I Could,

I would give you the World!

But all I can do is just offer you

MY LOVE!

My Love,

My Love

Is Pure, Unchanging, CRAZY!

My Love is just because Love!

I won't give you the Illusion that I am Perfect

But I will Forever give my all

When Loving you!

So, if this happens not to be enough for you.

Well, you know what you can do!

LEAVE!

GO!

SET ME FREE!

As all your Burdens, I have made my own

Be Released from me.

Please don't forget the Rocks of Insecurities

You have Thrown at my Soul

Planted in my Mind.

And Painted my body with!

Take this Dysfunctional Ass

Anger that Simmers in my Broken Heart!

I WANT NO PARTS!

It's time for me to heal,

So that my Foundation is Sturdy.

Only then will I be able to Build!

DON'T WORRY, I HAVE NOTHING TO RUN AND TELL!

I just sincerely wish YOU WELL!

I Promise to Tell the Truth.

The Whole Truth, the Plain Truth and Nothing

But the Truth So Help Me God!

It was a Cold, Rainy Day.

I drove ten minutes up the Road to my one-bedroom Box.

In my bet up Mobile.

There he laid in bed enjoying an Ice-Cold Beer.

No need for him to Work.

He knew I carried all the Weight.

He yelled out. "I'm hungry, hurry up!"

With 45 minutes left to spare before I was due back to Work,

I went right to the Kitchen to Cook his favorite meal.

It really was no big deal.

It was my Honor to Cater to him.

When he went out with the boys.

I'd remind him

I Love You Boo

But in return, he DIDN'T say I love you too.

Love don't Live Here Anymore.

Is the Whole Truth,

The Plain Truth and Nothing but the Truth!

It was me who Looked the other way.

Hoping the love I "thought" he had for me

Would soon come back one day.

Inflicting Abuse upon myself was staring back at me

In Plain Sight.

Yes, I Loved him with All My Might,

But I am Worth more than Gold. So, I have been told!

I asked him. Why do not you Just Leave and Let Me Be?

He replied: Well if I did, what would you do Without me?

Did he think he made me? Have him allowed him to feel such?

All the Punches turned into Pain, my constant Tears into Rain!

THE TRUTH WAS IN PLAIN SIGHT!

LEAVE!!!!

In the Wee Hours of the Night

As we slept so Peacefully.

I quietly moved his Arm away from me.

I packed my Bags without notice

Promised myself, I'd never become that Broken.

I learned that I ama Queen in Plain Sight

I now know that I deserve the Best

And that my friend is the Whole Truth,

The Plain Truth and Nothing but the Truth So Help Me God!

REFLECTION

Abuse comes in all forms!

Have you ever experienced abuse?

How does abuse affect the person you are today?

Have you ever inflicted abuse upon anyone else unintentionally?

Did you reconcile that? If so, how did you?

_____

_____

_____

_____

_____

_____

_____

_____

_____

_____

_____

_____

_____

WHO AM I?

WHO AM?

A 16-year-old girl trying to find my place in this world

An unwanted child

Abused, cold, left alone

Writing to keep from dying

Dying to keep from living

Living....living?

No, I can't be because I look myself directly in the Mirror

And screamed

Ugh! I Can't Stand Me!

I catch a Glimpse of me in my own Eyes

WHO AM I?

Walkin' down the street, grooving to my own Beat

A bet made him Explore my Body.

Looking into his Eyes,

DAMN, WHO AM I?

You're a Confused, Selfish Bitch

That's why I Kicked you in the Ditch

You ain't got enough Money and get in your Feelings

When another chick wants me.

Slap me, use me, Beat Me Down.

Still, I get sad as hell when you're not around.5, 6, 7, 8

Pretty soon, the years tell me it's too Late

BUT OH NO.

I wait around for your Validation

To pick me up off the Ground

You'd think I'd get tired of being let down.

Why don't I know

WHO AM I?

Walking. Talking, mommy, I Love You!

Not sure how to give my son the Best

There I go again, Settling for Less.

Take my Money, have my Pride

All I seem to do is Run and Hide!

WHO AM I?

Broken, Bruised, Cut, longing to be Healed.

God Blessed me with a wise old lady

Who stepped in and took the Wheel.

WHO AM I?

You're Beautiful, you're Bold

God Loves you, so you're NEVER Alone!

As I closed my Eyes and begin to Sleep

I slept in such harmony, for my GOD spoke to me!

You are a woman of God seeking my Face!

Don't ever stop your Chase!

I know your scorn, but I've declared this plan for you

Before you were even Born

You are more precious than Gold!

Walk like it

Talk like it

STAND FIRM IN IT!

You deserve all Desires of your Heart!

Which is way more than you have Inquired!

WHO ARE YOU?

YOU SAY!!!!

YOU'RE A QUEEN!

Now go lead the way!

I responded...YES I AM!!!!!

ABOUT THE AUTHOR

D ezarita Dashai is an author, poet and storyteller. She is a wife and mother of four boys.

Dezarita is the proud owner of Ms. Dezy House of Love childcare and founder of L.O.V.E nonprofit geared towards unaccompanied youth.

She enjoys basking in nature and listening to meaningful music of all genres.

Her motto is simply to put a smile on someone else face and help make the world a better place

Dezarita Dashai

www.ingramcontent.com/pod-product-compliance
Lightning Source LLC
Chambersburg PA
CBHW031230120626
46545CB00003B/1071